What People Are Saying About Joshua Mills an...

This is the season of the restoration of all things. Let it begin in you... revelation in his new book, *7 Divine Mysteries: Supernatural Secrets to Unlimited Abundance.*

—*Sid Roth*
Host, *It's Supernatural!*

Jesus said, *"I have come that they may have life, and that they may have it more abundantly"* (John 10:10), but many believers struggle to survive on a daily basis. The secret to an abundant life continues to remain a mystery to them. That is why I am so excited about the release of this new book by my good friend Joshua Mills, *7 Divine Mysteries: Supernatural Secrets to Unlimited Abundance.* Joshua lays out a clear, concise path for living a supernatural life with God's divine and supernatural provision. You will discover the spiritual keys to abundance and victory—no matter what your circumstances happen to be at the moment.

—*Joan Hunter*
Author and evangelist

I am so excited for you! *7 Divine Mysteries* is more than just a good book or a great read. It is a glorious God-invitation to step into the abundant life Jesus has provided for you—*a life of unlimited abundance!* God loves to share His secrets with His friends (see John 15:15). These friends of God are often the ones He chooses to not only share His divine mysteries with but also manifest the miracles of His mysteries in their lives in a way that creates a holy hunger for more of Him! When the apostle Paul spoke of those who would steward and distribute the divine mysteries of God throughout the earth, he pointed to a life of surrender and the fruit of faithfulness as necessary prerequisites (see 1 Corinthians 4:1–2). Joshua Mills is a friend of God, and in that place of friendship, faithfulness, and sacrificial surrender, God has imparted to him and his family beautiful truths and supernatural secrets to help you access the life of abundance that God has prepared for you.

—*Jason Hooper*
Senior Pastor, King's Way Church
www.kingswayal.com

In his new book, *7 Divine Mysteries: Supernatural Secrets to Unlimited Abundance*, Joshua Mills has pulled back the veil to uncover the secrets of living in plenitude. As a skilled musician uses musical notes to compose a masterpiece, Joshua uses written words to orchestrate God's glorious revelation of abundance. Filled with keen insight, powerful principles, and life-changing testimonies, this book will catapult you into another dimension of God's blessings.

—*Andrew Towe*
Lead Pastor, Ramp Church Chattanooga
Author, *The Triple Threat Anointing*

Joshua Mills does it again! *7 Divine Mysteries* is another must-have book that builds your faith, challenges your everyday thinking to go higher and deeper with God, and motivates you to press into the supernatural realm that is available to all of us. We love having Joshua minister at our church because not only is there a strong impartation of the supernatural power of God, but the body is encouraged to press into the Holy Spirit and experience the glory of God daily!

—*Mel and Desiree Ayres*
Pastors and Founders, In His Presence Church, Los Angeles
Producers of multiple music projects, including *Witness*
Author (Desiree Ayers), *Beyond the Flame* and *God Hunger*

STUDY GUIDE

7

DIVINE MYSTERIES

SUPERNATURAL SECRETS TO UNLIMITED ABUNDANCE

JOSHUA MILLS

WHITAKER
HOUSE

7 Divine Mysteries Study Guide:
Supernatural Secrets to Unlimited Abundance

International Glory Ministries
JoshuaMills.com
info@joshuamills.com

ISBN: 978-1-64123-764-2
eBook ISBN: 978-1-64123-765-9
Printed in the United States of America
© 2021 by Joshua Mills

Whitaker House
1030 Hunt Valley Circle
New Kensington, PA 15068
www.whitakerhouse.com

1 2 3 4 5 6 7 8 9 10 11 ᴨ 28 27 26 25 24 23 22 21

CONTENTS

INTRODUCTION

"You are permitted to understand the secrets of the Kingdom of Heaven...."
—Matthew 13:11 (NLT)

The *7 Divine Mysteries* book and study guide are the results of God's powerful revelation to me about the seven supernatural secrets concerning unlimited abundance. God revealed to me that manifesting abundance depends on my reliance on Him and Him alone. I desire for you to learn how to rest in this revelation also. A life of abundance is solely dependent upon living for Him and participating in agreement with His everlasting Word, the Bible—our life-giving source of truth and wisdom from the eternal God. I encourage you to take your time reading the book, absorbing new spiritual realities that you discover along the way. Then use this study guide to tap into God's unlimited abundance so you can walk in the blessings of heaven every day of your life.

These mysteries are supernatural secrets hidden from the natural mind—available only to those who are willing to operate by the mind of the Spirit. As these mysteries are unlocked for you in the book and then reinforced in this study guide, I believe you will begin to see them unlocked in your life, as you follow the leading of God's Spirit.

I'm excited to share with you what I have learned from the Spirit that will bring to life His desire for you to live an abundant life—today.

God's Spirit is inviting you to step into His realms of abundance and enjoy their benefits—but He won't force you. I pray that you will choose to move into what God is offering you. He will show up with

His sovereign presence and bring blessings, abundance, miracles, and breakthroughs if you open your heart and spirit to hear and obey His voice.

> *But you shall remember the* Lord *your **God, for it is He that gives you power to get wealth**, that He may establish His covenant which He swore to your fathers, as it is this day.* (Deuteronomy 8:18)

I love this Scripture passage from Deuteronomy because it teaches the secret of being successful in life. I call it "manifesting abundance," and this theme is found throughout the Scriptures. There is an entire realm of superabundance just waiting for you to explore it and put it to work. God is opening to His children untapped realms of overflowing provision.

Let's jump into this glory flow now by digging into each divine mystery and solving each one with God's Word, studying His wisdom, which has guided generations into abundant living.

HOW TO USE THIS STUDY GUIDE

This *7 Divine Mysteries Study Guide* can be used for either individual or group study. For your convenience, an answer key is provided at the back of this study guide. Notes pages are also included for recording your thoughts and testimonies about how God is touching your life through His divine mysteries.

TO FACILITATE PERSONAL STUDY

- Find a comfortable place and make it yours by playing peaceful instrumental worship music, which sets the atmosphere for receiving from the Spirit as you read and learn. (You may want to play some of my CDs or digital music downloads, especially *SpiritSpa* and *Experience His Glory*.)

- Always begin your time of study with a prayer, asking God to direct your thoughts and enable you to clearly understand the meaning of the words you read.

- There are eight lessons in this *7 Divine Mysteries Study Guide*. Feel free to pace yourself, but it is best to set a specific goal for finishing all the lessons, which will keep you moving forward. Momentum increases as you read through the lessons as each study builds upon the previous one.

- Remember to activate each lesson—applying it directly to your life as the Spirit ministers to you, engaging with the revelation you receive through your studies.

- Also remember that in every area of your life, God has a promise of victory! God has already established a promise of overcoming for you in His Word, the Bible. His abundance is at your disposal. Are you ready to learn how to receive it?

TO FACILITATE A STUDY GROUP

- Prepare your meeting space with peaceful, instrumental worship music to set a spiritual atmosphere before the group begins to gather. (You may want to use my CDs or digital music downloads, specifically *SpiritSpa* and *Experience His Glory.*)
- Always begin the meeting with a prayer, asking God to direct the conversation and bring divine understanding from the words that are read. As part of your prayer, you may want to speak this scriptural blessing over the group:

I keep asking that the God of our Lord Jesus Christ, the glorious Father, may give you the Spirit of wisdom and revelation, so that you may know him better. I pray that the eyes of your heart may be enlightened in order that you may know the hope to which he has called you, the riches of his glorious inheritance in his holy people, and his incomparably great power for us who believe. That power is the same as the mighty strength he exerted when he raised Christ from the dead and seated him at his right hand in the heavenly realms.

(Ephesians 1:17–10 NIV)

During the first meeting, have each person say their name and share their personal testimony in two minutes or less. Ask how they learned about the study group and/or why they are interested in learning about the *7 Divine Mysteries*. This helps the group become acquainted and feel more at ease to participate.

- At subsequent meetings, to begin the conversation, ask questions such as:
  - o "How did you like this week's chapter?"
  - o "Is there something from the book that you would especially like to discuss?"
  - o "Did anyone have a profound spiritual encounter since we last met?" (A financial miracle testimony, personal revelation, angelic experience, etc.) (I would love to hear about these encounters too—you may contact me at info@joshuamills.com.)
- Encourage group members to read the recommended pages from the *7 Divine Mysteries* book in advance, or ask people to take turns reading aloud, depending on time restrictions and/or personal preferences of the group.
- Try to keep the conversation centered on the book's content, but realize it may not be possible to cover all the points included in the study guide during each meeting. Don't feel pressured to complete all the points. Instead, see the study guide as a way of discovering divine abundance.
- It is important to allow the Spirit to direct your conversation, so focus on the areas that He is emphasizing through the group discussion of the lesson content.
- Choose a group activity so everyone can directly engage with the revelation within each lesson.
- To close the meeting, consider one or more of the following:
  - o Use the last point in the study guide.
  - o Pray a short prayer or ask another group member to do so.
  - o Together sing a worship song with a lesson-relevant theme.

- o Thank everyone for coming and let them know you are looking forward to seeing them again (state the day and time).
- Some group facilitators offer light refreshments at the end of the meeting to encourage fellowship and develop deeper community, providing an opportunity to continue discussions and add personal experiences. Group members may want to take turns providing refreshments. The host/hostess may want to make clear a time for ending the meeting as some conversations may get quite lengthy.
- You may want to schedule a special celebration after your last meeting to include a time of offering praise and worship, giving testimonies, and praying for one another, followed by refreshments and fellowship.

YOU CAN MANIFEST ABUNDANCE

"Then God blessed them and said, 'Be fruitful and multiply....'"
—Genesis 1:28 (NLT)

Before you begin this lesson, read Chapter 1 of *7 Divine Mysteries*.

SUPERNATURAL MYSTERIES 101

1. As a "spiritual" detective seeking to uncover the supernatural mysteries that God has given you in His Word and revealed through His Spirit, what are the first few questions you need to ask?

    • What is the _____ of divine _____?

    • What are the foundational _____ that apply to all _____ mysteries of _____?

    • What further clues will _____ their _____?

2. God confirms in the Bible and in testimonies of people's lives today that His supernatural provision is real. List three Bible passages you are familiar with that confirm His supernatural provision, and then write a testimony—yours or another's—that also confirms His provision.

1. _____

2. _____

3. _____

_____

_____

_____

ABUNDANCE COMES FROM HEAVEN

3. When you have a financial need, where do you usually place your focus? Check all that apply:

_____ Your checking account

_____ Your savings account

_____ A bank where you might obtain a loan

_____ The want ads

_____ The resources of family or friends

_____ People in the news who are wealthy

_____ The lottery or a casino

_____ An e-commerce website

_____ Heavenward, looking to the Lord

4. In the loaves and fish story in Matthew 14, where was Jesus's focus before He blessed and broke and gave the loaves to His disciples?

_____

_____

OVERFLOWING SPAGHETTI

5. Do you have an "overflowing spaghetti"-type story? Even if it wasn't as plentiful as feeding more than five thousand people, as Jesus did, or even the dozen or so people, as told in the book, was there a time when God supernaturally provided you with something when you least expected it? If so, write about it.

_____

_____

_____

ABUNDANCE FOR EVERY NEED

6. As a believer, you know that financial wealth isn't the most accurate definition of true abundance. With that in mind, write your personal-specific definition of true abundance:

_____

_____

_____

ABUNDANCE IS A COMMAND

7. Where in the Bible is the first divine instruction to manifest abundance?

_____

ABUNDANCE IS A GIFT

8. *"And you shall _____ the LORD your God, for it is He who gives you _____ to get wealth, that He may establish His covenant..."* (_____ _____).

9. Of all the wealth available to you, what abundance would you like to receive first? Why?

_____

_____

_____

ABUNDANCE IS ACCESSED THROUGH ABIDING AND RECEIVING

10. Throughout the Bible (and throughout the ages following), we see humans continually falling short of the glory and will of God. Can you relate to the following people's downfalls—and to some of them subsequently returning to God through His mercy and grace? Check all that apply:

_____ Adam and Eve (deception; Genesis 3:1–5)

_____ Abraham (lying; Genesis 20:2)

_____ Sarah (jealousy; Genesis 16:4–6)

_____ Israelites (impatience; Exodus 32:1)

_____ David (lust; 2 Samuel 11:1–4)

_____ Peter (fear; Luke 22:52–62)

_____ Judas (greed; Matthew 27:3)

11. Some people are conservative when it comes to "lifting hands into the realms of glory," as I wrote about in _7 Divine Mysteries._ Have you tried this expression of worship? If so, what was your experience?

_____

_____

_____

12. Do you believe that raising your hands in worship is a necessary part of offering yourself as a "living sacrifice"? In your reading of the Bible, have you seen any scriptural precedents for this?

_____

_____

_____

13. Write what the following statements mean to you: "God's creative glory resides within you through His Spirit, and He will release that creative glory through your hands.... Your hands will become supernatural portals for God's power to flow out through you, releasing divine creativity connected with receiving abundance in all spheres of life."

_____

_____

_____

PURIFYING YOUR HANDS

14. *"Who shall _____ into the hill of the LORD? or who shall _____ in His holy place? He that has _____ _____, and a _____ _____; who has not lifted up his soul to vanity, nor sworn deceitfully"* (Psalm 24:3–4).

15. How have you used your hands recently to assist, bless, or give to others?

_____

_____

16. Are you holding on to so much "junk" that your hands can't carry the love of God to others? Write what may be preventing your hands from reaching out to praise God and help others.

_____

_____

_____

ABUNDANCE IS ACTIVATED BY FAITH

17. God is often waiting for us to move in faith toward His promises! What happens when true faith is established in your heart?

_____

PRIORITIZING OUR FINANCES

18. Seven financial areas need to be prioritized in your life—each is vital when stewarding the abundance God has blessed you with. Place the following in the correct order, with 1 being the most important and 7 the least: Bills; Save; Necessities; Debt; Tithe/give/sow; Tax; Luxuries

    1. _____

    2. _____

    3. _____

    4. _____

    5. _____

    6. _____

    7. _____

WORSHIP IN SPIRIT AND TRUTH

19. God's revelation concerning worship and its power to change your life and circumstances, and worshipping God in Spirit and in truth, causes you to feel His joy, goodness, and glory. Then, the angels of heaven will gather to join you. Why does this happen?

_____

_____

_____

20. *"Honor the Lord with your* _____ *and with the* _____ _____ *of everything you produce. Then* _____ _____ _____ *your barns with grain, and your vats will* _____ *with good wine"* (Proverbs 3:9–10 Nlt).

ACTIVATIONS

1. The book mentions several areas where people may need a miracle: health, business, relationship, etc. Do you need a miracle today? Repeat the following with conviction and confidence: **"I am reaching up for what You have already provided for me, God, and I receive it now! You are wonderful, Lord, and I take hold of the fullness of Your wonder right now. Thank You!"**

2. List ten ways you can bless others with your hands. Then commit to following through with one each day for the next ten days. (Examples: hug at least five people in one day; write an encouraging letter to a relative; open the door for someone, etc.)

   _____

   _____

   _____

   _____

   _____

   _____

   _____

   _____

   _____

   _____

3. If you are in debt for luxuries, I encourage you to seek financial help with a reputable Christian person or organization. Diligently and seriously research the Internet or ask someone you know who is financially solvent to show you ways to pay off that debt and follow a godly budget.

NOTES

NOTES

NOTES

NOTES

NOTES

DIVINE MYSTERY #1: HEAVENLY VISION IS A PATHWAY FOR PROVISION

"Beloved, I pray that in every way you may succeed and prosper and be in good health [physically], just as [I know] your soul prospers [spiritually]."
—3 John 1:2 (AMP)

Before you begin this lesson, read chapter 2, "Divine Mystery #1," of 7 *Divine Mysteries*.

Which of the following Scriptures touches your heart and spirit in a special way? After each, write what you feel the Spirit is specifically telling you about how you can weave this Scripture into your daily walk on the pathway of provision and abundance.

And you shall remember the Lord *your God, for it is He who gives you power to get wealth, that He may establish His covenant which He swore to your fathers, as it is this day.*

(Deuteronomy 8:18 NKJV)

_____

_____

_____

By His stripes we are healed. (Isaiah 53:5 NKJV)

_____

_____

_____

And the floors shall be full of wheat, and the vats shall overflow with wine and oil. (Joel 2:24)

_____

_____

_____

So your barns will be filled with plenty, and your vats will overflow with new wine.

(Proverbs 3:10 NKJV)

_____

_____

_____

Honor the Lord *with your possessions, and with the firstfruits of all your increase.*

(Proverbs 3:9 NKJV)

_____

_____

_____

Honor the LORD with your wealth and with the best part of everything you produce. Then he will fill your barns with grain, and your vats will overflow with good wine. (Proverbs 3:9 NLT)

_____

_____

_____

I came that they may have and enjoy life, and have it in abundance [to the full, till it overflows]. (John 10:10 AMP)

_____

_____

_____

Then God blessed them and said, "Be fruitful and multiply…." (Genesis 1:28 NLT)

_____

_____

_____

Then He commanded the multitudes to sit down on the grass. And He took the five loaves and the two fish, and looking up to heaven, He blessed and broke and gave the loaves to the disciples; and the disciples gave to the multitudes. So they all ate and were filled, and they took up twelve baskets full of the fragments that remained. Now those who had eaten were about five thousand men, besides women and children. (Matthew 14:19–21 NKJV)

_____

_____

_____

They are like trees planted along the riverbank, bearing fruit each season. Their leaves never wither, and they prosper in all they do. (Psalm 1:3 NLT)

_____

_____

_____

Do not be deceived, God is not mocked; for whatever a man sows, that he will also reap.

(Galatians 6:7 NKJV)

_____

_____

_____

Whoever sows to please their flesh, from the flesh will reap destruction; whoever sows to please the Spirit, from the Spirit will reap eternal life. Let us not become weary in doing good, for at the proper time we will reap a harvest if we do not give up ["do not lose heart" NKJV]. (Galatians 6:8–9 NIV)

_____

_____

_____

The blessing of the LORD makes one rich, and He adds no sorrow with it. (Proverbs 10:22 NKJV)

_____

_____

_____

My God shall supply all your need according to His riches in glory by Christ Jesus.

(Philippians 4:19 NKJV)

_____

_____

_____

Where there is no vision, the people perish.   (Proverbs 29:18 KJV)

_____

_____

_____

1. The Bible says, *"Where there is no vision, the people perish"* (Proverbs 29:18 KJV). In this day, we must receive _____ _____; when we do, instead of _____, we will begin _____.

REALIZE THIS: "DANGER WILL NOT COME NEAR YOU"

2. Psalm 91:9–10 says, *"Because you have made _____ _____, _____ _____ _____ _____, even the Most High, your dwelling place, _____ _____ _____ _____ _____, nor will any plague come near your tent"* (AMP).

3. God said, *"A thousand may fall at your side and ten thousand at your right hand, but **danger will not come near you**"* (Psalm 91:7 AMP). Write the top four dangers you fear today. Then write a declaration for each based on God's Word that dispels your fears and places God in control, and state them out loud.

_____

_____

_____

_____

4. You can _____ _____ _____ of the enemy by _____

    _____ _____ and His Word.

5. Write as many words as come to mind that describe a dwelling place or refuge:

    _____

    _____

    _____

    Now write several reasons why you should make God your refuge, your dwelling place.

    _____

    _____

    _____

6. Have you allowed glory realm realities to become your heavenly vision? Why or why not?

    _____

    _____

    _____

7. The beautiful thing about having a _____ is that it keeps you moving forward.... When
    God gives us a vision of His _____, it moves us away from _____ and
    toward His _____.

    Have you unraveled the mystery of how to maintain your journey on the pathway of abundance
    God designed for you before you were born?

    _____

    _____

    _____

8. Angels attend to our every need. They come to _____, _____, and _____ us, and they will do much more as we learn to _____ _____ them and _____ _____ _____ _____ on our behalf.

RECOGNIZE GOD'S PLANS TO PROSPER YOU

9. List many gifts from God you have received to date and some you hope to receive in the future:

_____

_____

_____

10. What does the following verse mean to you? *"Beloved, I pray that **in every way you may succeed and prosper** and be in good health [physically], just as [I know] your soul prospers [spiritually]"* (3 John 1:2 AMP). Pray for God's revelation and then write the verse in your own words:

_____

_____

_____

ENVISION A CHANNEL OF BLESSINGS

11. True prosperity is having enough to meet your own needs with enough left over to meet the needs of someone else. Why are some churches opposed to prosperity? What are your views?

_____

_____

_____

12. Psalm 35:27 says, *"Let them shout for _____ and be _____, who favor my _____ _____; and let them say continually, 'Let _____ _____ be magnified, who has _____ _____ _____ _____ _____ of His servant.'"*

13. Real prosperity starts in your spirit, but it then flows to your soul and ultimately manifests in your physical body and through your finances. How would you define "real prosperity," or abundance, in your spirit, soul, physical body, and finances? Do so here:

_____

_____

_____

14. Deuteronomy 8:17–18 says, *"…the LORD your **God**, for it is He who **gives you power to get wealth**, that He may establish His covenant which He swore to your fathers, as it is this day"* (NKJV). Do you believe in your heart this promise from God is for you? What kind of wealth is He referring to?

_____

_____

_____

15. Can you think of some things that you've held on to for a while but are no longer improving your quality of life? Would you be willing to seek the Lord and ask Him how He would have you to release them? As you receive revelation, write a small list here.

_____

_____

_____

NUMBERS AS SUPERNATURAL SIGNS

16. Have you been noticing number repetition occurring frequently in your life? If so, has the Spirit been prophetically speaking to you through it? Which specific numbers have you noticed, and how has God been speaking to you?

_____

_____

17. *"And you shall _____ the* L ORD *your God, for it is He who gives you _____ to*

    get _____, that He may establish His covenant which He swore to your fathers, as it is this day"

    (Deuteronomy 8:18 NKJV).

TO SEAL THE TRUTH IN YOUR SPIRIT

18. What promise will you be repeating every day for seven days? What are you expecting to happen?
    Do you really *know* that every word of it is true? After writing out your promise, daily speak it
    aloud. Believe.

    _____

    _____

    _____

19. What is the difference between thinking that God *owes* you abundant life and believing God
    promises you abundant life? (See John 10:10; Jeremiah 11:29; Deuteronomy 30:20; Mark 10:21; Luke
    18:22 AMP.)

    _____

    _____

    _____

DECREES OF ABUNDANCE

20. Referring to the decrees found at the end of chapter 2, "Divine Mystery #1," in the book, write
    how these seven decrees based on God's Word will change your life when God's promised
    abundance manifests.

    _____

    _____

    _____

ACTIVATIONS

1. Think of someone over whom you can shower abundance in a meaningful way. Perhaps an ill cousin would welcome a get-well card, flowers, and a prayer delivered by you in person. How about giving a child your undivided attention during a one-on-one game or activity? Or paying for a coworker's portion of the coffee fund for a month? The list is endless. Take time to think about a plan and then activate it on your pathway to prosperity and abundance.

2. Write what you believe would be a heavenly vision from God that leads you on a journey to abundance, whether that would be an overflow of finances, good health, friendships, career advancement, volunteer opportunities, etc. Then act on it!

3. Following the example of feasting in Divine Mystery #1, when possible, buy extra groceries and then bundle them together and gift the goodies, expecting nothing in return, to a neighbor, church member, pastor, friend, or family member—surprise someone with the blessing of God's bounty. There are many food pantries and organizations that would appreciate a helping hand. Every act of kindness is a step ahead on the pathway of provision.

NOTES

NOTES

NOTES

NOTES

LESSON 3

DIVINE MYSTERY #2: WHAT YOU SAY CREATES A WAY

"For by your words you will be justified, and by your words you shall be condemned."
—Matthew 12:37

Before you begin this lesson, read chapter 3, "Divine Mystery #2," of *7 Divine Mysteries*.

SPEAKING IN FAITH

1. Do you or someone you know have a story similar to my early "speaking in faith" experience described in the *7 Divine Mysteries* book? If so, briefly describe it.

_____

_____

2. What is Jesus telling us in Mark 11:23?

    Truly I tell you, if anyone says to this mountain, "Go, throw yourself into the sea," and does not doubt in their heart but believes that what they say will happen, it will be done for them. (NIV)

    _____

    _____

    _____

3. Speaking in faith is choosing to direct divine activity around your life. How willing are you to put this divine mystery to work?
    Circle one: Totally willing – Somewhat willing – Maybe willing
    In which area of your life—physical, financial, spiritual, or relational—would you first like to put speaking in faith into practice?

    _____

    _____

    _____

4. *"And God* _____ _____ *to bless you abundantly, so that in all things at all times, having all that you need,* _____ _____ _____ *in every good work"* (2 Corinthians 9:8 NIV).

5. Regardless of what it looks like in the natural, God has promised _____ and _____, and they are available to you _____ _____.

    Are you ready to receive? List what you are prepared for and willing to receive from God today.

    _____

    _____

    _____

WHAT ARE YOU THINKING?

6. What we say _____ a way, but what we _____ starts in our minds and emotions.
    Pray that the Holy Spirit will filter what you think and say through His mercy and grace.

RECOGNIZE YOUR TRUE ENEMIES AND RECOGNIZE WHERE YOU DWELL

7. In what areas of your life have you been dealing with the enemies (the *"spiritual forces of wickedness"*) that are described in Ephesians 6:12?

    _____

    _____

    _____

8. Explain each of the following:

    First heaven: _____

    Second heaven: _____

    Third heaven: _____

9. In which heaven are you seated according to Ephesians 2:6?

    _____

    _____

    _____

REJECTING THE REALM OF LIES

10. The enemy spirit is committed to destroying you. This has been his desire from the time of Eden. Write John 8:44 in your own words, taking seriously what it means to have such an enemy.

_____

_____

_____

PROMOTE GOD'S TRUTH IN THE CHURCH

11. Reflecting on the past, can you trace how the enemy has attempted to use lies and deceit to damage the body of Christ?

_____

_____

_____

12. Perhaps you have a relationship that is on the rocks, so to speak. Have you prayerfully considered that the enemy spirit may be placing devious thoughts of envy, rivalry, or selfish ambition in your mind or the other person's mind? Remember, _____ leads to lack, but _____ _____ leads to abundance.

Matthew 5:9 says, _"Blessed are the peacemakers: for they shall be called the children of God."_ Expand on how this verse applies to you personally.

_____

_____

_____

KNOW THE TRUTH ABOUT YOUR ANOINTING

13. If the enemy has tried to destroy your God-given gift (hospitality, teaching, etc.), in what ways has he succeeded? In what ways have you thwarted his mission? What action have you taken to keep from believing his lies?

_____

_____

_____

14. Deep down, you know that God is the only One who really knows you. When you speak His truth, His Word, the enemy will flee. Jesus is our example. Read Matthew 4:1–11 and then write what you will say the next time the enemy tempts you.

_____

_____

_____

LIVING IN THE REALM OF TRUTH

15. Do you seek and say the truth in all circumstances? Do you firmly believe that choosing God's truth is "the greatest spiritual warfare _____ you have at your disposal" and that it brings "you _____ in _____ _____"?

PROCLAIM THE TRUTH THROUGH PRAISE

16. When you determine to focus solely on the truth, what you say and do will create a way to topple every wall and barrier you are facing and will face in the future. _"Then _____ _____ _____ to Joshua, 'See, _____ _____ _____ Jericho into your hands...'"_ (Joshua 6:2 NIV).

17. Joshua listened to the voice of the Lord. What is your heavenly Father saying to you today? Will you follow through, even though it may seem strange to others?

_____

_____

_____

DECREE WHAT YOU NEED

18. If you haven't already answered these questions from the book, take time now to pray about them, and then answer them thoughtfully and honestly:

    Do I understand who my real enemies are? _____

    Do I understand who and what to believe? _____

    Do I understand how to position my faith? _____

    What am I speaking? _____

    What am I decreeing? _____

    What am I declaring? _____

    What sounds am I releasing? _____

19. You may have a prophetic utterance in your spirit, prompted by the Holy Spirit. What is revelation in the heavens becomes prophetic on earth; and when you have it in your mouth and say it, it brings forth an anointing in the atmosphere that ushers in the abundant glory of God. What revelation does God want you to bring forth today?

_____

_____

_____

20. The *"great shout"* that caused the walls of Jericho to come down is within you—a gift from God. As you decree God's truths, expect to begin manifesting overflowing abundance—so much more than "just enough." What is the first manifestation you expect? Write what it is and why you desire it first.

_____

_____

_____

ACTIVATIONS

1. Think of a place where you can be totally alone and quiet with no distractions. Plan a time to go there to pray, listen for God, and then let out a *"great shout"* of praise and worship to bring down any wall that's keeping you from God's abundance.

2. Write a prayer from your heart to your heavenly Father, telling Him how you will not listen to the enemy's lies and will only believe His truth. List specific personal circumstances that may be affecting you currently or are bothering you from the past.

_____

_____

_____

3. Of the following truths, which one can you bring alive today with deliberate actions? Make it so.
   - From the abundance of my heart flows the abundance of God's blessings.
   - Every word I speak is anointed to create my future reality.
   - I will guard my lips and only allow God's truth to flow from my mouth.
   - As I speak God's Word, God's Word speaks back to me.
   - I live in the truth, I speak the truth, and I walk into the truth.
   - I am seated in heavenly places with Christ Jesus and abundance flows through me.
   - I am anointed to carry God's abundant overflow everywhere I go.

NOTES

NOTES

NOTES

DIVINE MYSTERY #3: THE WORD YOU WORK WILL WORK FOR YOU

*"**All Scripture is God-breathed** [given by divine inspiration] and is **profitable for instruction**, for **conviction** [of sin], for **correction** [of error and restoration to obedience], for **training** in righteousness [learning to live in conformity to God's will, both publicly and privately—**behaving** honorably with personal **integrity** and moral courage]; so that the man of God may be complete and proficient, **outfitted** and thoroughly **equipped** for every good work."*
—2 Timothy 3:16–17 (AMP)

Before you begin this lesson, read chapter 4, "Divine Mystery #3," of *7 Divine Mysteries.*

1. Every time you read the Scriptures—the Bible, God's Word—a new doorway with heavenly illumination will open with an invitation for you to step in and receive God and all He has for you. There are various Bible versions today. Which version is your favorite? _____

Why are you drawn to that version?

_____

_____

2. God's Word lights your path and waters your soul. What darkness in your life needs His light, and what dry areas in your soul need to be watered? Pray about these matters and then write your answers.

_____

_____

_____

3. As with Pastor Lowder's tomato plant, do you sometimes feel withered and fruitless? How can God's Word bring you back to life? What Scriptures speak about life? List a few and meditate on each of them.

_____

_____

_____

WORKING WITH GOD'S WORD

4. God's Word overcomes _____, _____, _____, _____, and _____. His Word floods _____ and _____ with _____ _____. His Word overcomes _____ with the flow of _____ _____.

5. What must happen for a revelation to produce a manifestation?

_____

_____

_____

6. God is looking for those who will simply _____ His Word, _____ the _____ of it, and _____ to it…. We are to be _____ of the Word, and in *doing the Word*—participating, working, and fully engaging with it—we will produce the _____ of the Word.

START WHERE YOU ARE AND WORK WITH WHAT YOU HAVE

7. Where are you on the sowing and reaping spectrum? Have you begun to sow seeds? Are you looking forward to an abundant harvest? Or have you only been thinking about sowing and harvesting? What steps will you take today to begin the process?

    _____

    _____

    _____

8. *"Remember this: Whoever sows sparingly will also reap sparingly, and whoever sows generously will also reap generously"* (2 Corinthians 9:6 NIV). Does this verse in God's Word *intimidate* you or *motivate* you? Circle the word that best describes your reaction, then check the answer key.

    _____

    _____

    _____

9. Write your thoughts about my receiving an overflow of abundance from a completely unexpected source in response to my obedience and commitment to God's law of multiplication.

    _____

    _____

    _____

10. Psalm 91:11 says, *"For He will command His angels in regard to you, to protect and defend and guard you in all your ways [of obedience and service]"* (AMP). Do you rely on God's angels for protection?

    _____ Yes   _____ No

    If yes, why? Have you felt their presence protecting you from harm?

    _____

    _____

    If no, explain:

    _____

    _____

11. I believe that God gives angels assignments to keep us safe in all our ways, which makes angels our servants. Do you agree? Explain.

    _____

    _____

    _____

12. God's Word, the Bible, says His children can search out and understand His mysteries—things that humans cannot know or discover unless God reveals it to them. As a child of God, have you received helpful revelation from the Holy Spirit? _____ If so, write about it here:

    _____

    _____

    _____

13. God's Word tells us that angels are assigned to us. There are angels surrounding you, specifically placed by Him to work with you. How intrigued are you about angels, God's messengers? Circle one and explain your choice: Very intrigued – Somewhat intrigued – Not intrigued

_____

_____

_____

14. From the very beginning, God created everything we see with His spoken word. Today, He is speaking to us about the angelic realm and the benefits angels can bring to our daily lives. Are you willing to accept this revelation and welcome angelic assistance?

_____

_____

_____

15. I believe strongly that God wants His children to become more aware of their assigned angels. The armies of angels, the hosts of heaven, are at our disposal. What types of battles do you envision your angels fighting for you?

_____

_____

_____

16. Why isn't the Holy Spirit a replacement for the ministry of angels?

_____

_____

_____

17. While God's angels have a purpose, what are three cautions that we must be aware of when interacting with the ministry of angels?

_____

_____

_____

WORD-BASED PRAISE LEADS TO REVELATION

18. God desires to bring manifestations to your life—manifestations of _____, manifestations of _____, manifestations of _____, manifestations of _____. He wants to release many kinds of manifestations, but they will only come as you allow the Spirit to bring you _____. There are downloads of _____, _____, and _____ _____ waiting for you in heaven. Will you receive these revelations and rise up into the Spirit realms to do new things?

_____

_____

_____

19. God wants to take you places in the Spirit that will forever change you, what you say, and what you do. When you have a revelation of something through God's Word, if you see it and ask for it, you can have it. List some Scripture passages that confirm this truth.

_____

_____

_____

20. A thousand years before Jesus went to the cross, David already knew that God's Son would

pay the price for our _____ _____ _____ _____, that He would

_____ ____ _____ _____, that He would _____

_____ _____ from destruction, that He would _____ ____ with

lovingkindness and tender mercies, that He would _____ our mouths with good

things so that our _____ ____ _____ like the eagle's.

ACTIVATIONS

1. Choose a verse or two from God's Word and allow it to work for you as you absorb it into your heart and memorize it with your mind. Psalm 103:1–5 is a good place to start.

2. Research the instances when God uses angels to assist, warn, inform, and protect people in the Old Testament and the New Testament. I have included a list of Scriptures in my book *Seeing Angels*, Appendix II, "Angels in the Bible—394 Scripture References."

3. Make a list of areas in your life in which you would like God to move. Which Scriptures will you use to begin working the Word to see transformation in these areas? Fill in the chart on the next page.

Personal Area of Need	Working the Word
1.	
2.	
3.	
4.	
5.	
6.	
7.	
8.	
9.	
10.	
11.	
12.	
13.	
14.	
15.	

NOTES

NOTES

DIVINE MYSTERY #4: WHAT YOU SOW, YOU WILL GROW

*"My **God shall supply all your need** according to His riches in glory by Christ Jesus."*
—Philippians 4:19

Before you begin this lesson, read chapter 5, "Divine Mystery #4," of 7 *Divine Mysteries*.

1. This chapter begins with a promise from God that is "available for those who will say…." How many of the following declarations do you say in response to God's promise? Check all that apply:

   _____ Yes, Lord, I will respond to Your call.

   _____ I will rise up and let my light shine.

   _____ I will share the gospel.

   _____ I will be a soul winner.

   _____ I will be a miracle worker.

_____ I will do what You said I could do in this hour.

_____ I will rely on the Greater One inside me.

_____ God is greater than anyone or anything.

_____ God is greater than any recession or any sickness.

_____ God is already taking care of all my needs.

_____ Jesus has already won my battles.

_____ I continually declare victory over my life because of what Jesus accomplished.

PLANTING OUR SEEDS FOR GOD'S GLORY

2. The following spiritual seeds have distinctive characteristics:

_____ is a seed for longevity.

_____ is a seed for understanding.

_____ is a seed for emotional and physical healing.

_____ is a seed for righteousness.

_____ is a seed that opens doors of opportunity.

_____ is a seed that produces peace.

_____ _____ is a seed that produces financial harvest.

3. Of the seven seeds you just identified, which two are easiest, most natural, for you to plant?

_____

_____

_____

_____

Which two are the hardest, pushing you out of your comfort zone?

_____

_____

_____

_____

Now, write about the one you will concentrate on the most over the next week, planting as many seeds as possible.

_____

_____

_____

_____

PLANTING IN GOOD SOIL

4. Have you experienced problems with the seed you have sown not yielding a return, just as the woman mentioned in the book experienced? Why is it important to sow into good soil?

_____

_____

_____

5. Describe *"good ground"* (Matthew 13:8 NKJV). What is another name for good ground?

_____

_____

_____

GOD SOIL AND THE MIRACLE SEED

6. God _____ with a God _____ produces a God _____. God soil is _____ ground that produces _____ results—wonderful fruitfulness and multiplication.

7. Galatians 6:7 says, *"Do not be deceived, God is not mocked; for whatever a man sows, that he will also reap"* (NKJV). When you sow the Word of God, you will reap the harvest of that Word. What does this mean to you?

   _____

   _____

   _____

8. You can plant the Word of God as a _____ _____ in your _____ and then watch it grow. Over the days and weeks and months of the year in which we read the _____, miracle seeds are being deposited into our _____, and they are not placed there to die. They have not been planted there to get choked out by the cares of the world. God planted them with the anticipation of watching each one grow and flourish, providing a _____ in your life.

9. Books written by Ruth Ward Heflin and Charles and Frances Hunter have made a huge difference in my life. Have you had a similar experience while reading Spirit-filled books? What title(s) come to mind when you think of books that have made an impact on your life?

   _____

   _____

   _____

62

10. Have you ever wanted to *do* something for God that consumed your thoughts and spirit? If so, what was it, and did you actually follow through and do it?

   _____

   _____

   If not, why do you think that is?

   _____

   _____

11. How do you define the word *steward*?

   _____

   _____

   When it comes to being a good "steward" of God's revelations and resources, how would you rate yourself?

   ____ Excellent

   ____ Very good

   ____ Good

   ____ I am willing to learn and improve

12. Have you been holding back from releasing your God-given abilities to bless others? What gifts do you have and how can you share them? List your gifts and then list ways you can share each with specific people (name two).

   _____

   _____

13. What seeds do you have in your heart and hands that need to be scattered far and wide? How can you spread them? Prayerfully ponder these two questions and write what God reveals to you.

_____

_____

_____

14. What does the supernatural secret and spiritual principle *You must sow whatever you desire to grow* mean to you?

_____

_____

_____

15. In all honesty, *what do you desire to grow?*

_____

_____

Does your desire line up with God's desire?

_____

_____

FIVE SUPERNATURAL SECRETS ABOUT MONEY

16. _____ is an important _____ that God wants us to have so that _____ _____ can flow to us and the word through us.

17. _____ identifies the true _____ of your _____. *"For where your* _____ *is, there will your* _____ *be also"* (Matthew 6:21).

18. _____ should always be used to _____ _____, who is the Source of overflowing abundance.

19. _____ is a tool for _____ _____.

20. _____ always _____ a _____ _____. A spirit of poverty attempts to keep God's people bound in chains of lack. But! The Bible is clear that God gives you the ability to become prosperous: *"And you shall remember the _____ _____ _____, for it is He who _____ _____ power to get _____..."* (Deuteronomy 8:18 NKJV).

ACTIVATIONS

1. Take inventory of all the revelations and resources God has abundantly blessed you with; if you did not rate yourself as being an "Excellent" steward, decide what steps you will take to become a better steward of God's resources in your life. Begin to take those steps today.

2. Of the seven seeds identified, what seeds will you sow to grow? What tools and resources do you need to use to ensure the seed will take root and mature?

3. Choose to receive the impartation prayer for physical healing, financial provision, relationship breakthrough, a resolution to a family matter, restoration, justice, or whatever else you need. Write exactly the steps you will take as part of embracing the promise of a flourishing harvest in your life.

NOTES

NOTES

NOTES

NOTES

NOTES

DIVINE MYSTERY #5: GENEROUS BELIEVING PRODUCES GENEROUS RECEIVING

*"**Give, and it will be given to you**. A good measure, pressed down,*
shaken together and running over, will be poured into your lap.
For with the measure you use, it will be measured to you."
—Luke 6:38 (NIV)

Before you begin this lesson, read chapter 6, " Divine Mystery #5," of 7 *Divine Mysteries.*

1. _____ and then _____ _____ from God's abundance go hand in hand.

2. When you believe God's Word about giving and receiving, you must receive as generously as you give. Answer the following questions honestly after pausing to think about each:

How gracious are you when it comes to receiving?

_____

_____

Do you accept a compliment with a smile and a "Thank you"? Or do you mumble and try to deflect the gift?

_____

_____

Do you feel you don't need anybody's help in your life and therefore refuse gifts and offers of assistance?

_____

_____

Have you struggled with the spirit of poverty?

_____

_____

3. God wants you to receive His abundance with a grateful heart and open mind. Does a Scripture come to mind as you think about His generosity?

_____

_____

RECEIVE HIS ABUNDANCE

4. Matthew 6:33 says, *"Seek the Kingdom of God above all else, and live righteously, and he will give you everything you need"* (NLT). Is discovering, focusing on, and aiming at the kingdom of God at the top of your priority list? If not, what has replaced your top priority?

_____

5. Why does God want to bless you? Because He loves you—so much so that He suffered pain and agony, bled, and died for you. He was thinking about you while hanging on the cross. Do you believe and receive that reality?

_____

_____

_____

6. Out of the overflow of God's _____ for you, He wants to _____ _____ with abundance. I urge you to accept _____ _____ with _____, praise, and _____.

SEVEN LEVELS OF SUPERNATURAL RECEIVING

LEVEL 1: "GIVE, AND IT WILL BE GIVEN TO YOU"

7. How open are you to receiving abundance that may come as supernatural surprises? Name a few expected and unexpected ways God may gift you with abundance.

_____

_____

_____

8. Have you or someone you know received financial abundance that was obviously a supernatural money miracle?

_____

_____

_____

LEVEL 2: *"GOOD MEASURE"*

9. God has destined you for good measure, or increase in every area of your life. Where would you like to see an increase today? Check all that apply, then believe and receive and bless others:

____ Physical

____ Spiritual

____ Financial

____ Relational

____ Emotional

____ Family

____ Career

10. Our God is the Spirit of _____, and He wants the realm of _____ _____ to flow in and _____ _____ _____ every day.

LEVEL 3: *"PRESSED DOWN"*

11. God's glory realms are filled with blessing. One Hebrew word translated as "glory" is *kabod*. What does this word mean?

_____

_____

_____

12. Being "pressed down" physically may make you think of being tired and worn out. But this level of blessing from God is the intense pressure of knowing how much He loves and cares for you, and how much He has blessed you. Do you feel it? Express it:

_____

_____

_____

LEVEL 4: *"SHAKEN TOGETHER"*

13. Having childlike faith is mentioned in the Bible, and Jesus says in Matthew 19:14, *"Let the little children come to Me, and do not forbid them; for of such is the kingdom of heaven"* (NKJV). How does this attitude of faith reflect Lincoln's story in the book?

_____

_____

_____

14. God wants you to be a _____ _____ so you can then be an extraordinary, extravagant, and _____ _____ too.

LEVEL 5: *"RUNNING OVER"*

15. What does it mean to you that there is "an overflow of abundance in the realm of the Spirit"?

_____

_____

_____

16. Being generous with a little teaches us how to be generous with a lot. Rate your current level of giving by circling one:

Extravagant – Very Generous – Generous – Moderately Generous – Learning to be generous

LEVEL 6: *"POURED INTO YOUR LAP"*

17. Level 6 speaks of _____ and _____ prosperity, as well as of divine _____, _____, and _____.

18. Have you been divinely connected with people who brought with them God's abundance? Did you recognize it immediately, or did you realize after a period of time that God had orchestrated the entire meeting and outcome? Remember it here in writing:

_____

_____

_____

LEVEL 7: "WITH THE MEASURE YOU USE, IT WILL BE MEASURED TO YOU"

19. *"So let's not get tired of _____ what is _____. At just the right time we will _____ a harvest of _____ if we _____ _____ _____"* (Galatians 6:9 NLT).

20. God has prepared massive fruitfulness just for you. The key is that you must continue moving in the things of God and allowing the things of God to move through you. How can you keep moving forward in the Spirit so you can enter into God's abundance?

_____

_____

_____

Generously receive God's abundance—practice the art of being a grateful child who graciously receives from their generous Father.

ACTIVATIONS

1. Commit to thanking God for ten blessings every day before getting out of bed.

2. Choose to bless a child one day and to bless an adult on another day. Take note of the reactions of each, including the differences between them that may be obvious and those that may be more subtle. Then be aware of your own reaction when God chooses to bless you.

3. If you (or others) consider yourself to be a stockpiler, take inventory of your living area and/or workplace and give away or toss items that you *know* you will never need or use. If this process is overwhelming for you, pray and ask the Holy Spirit to give you the strength and determination to break the habit of stockpiling and make a clean sweep!

NOTES

NOTES

NOTES

NOTES

NOTES

DIVINE MYSTERY #6: ANGEL POWER MAKES ABUNDANCE SHOWER

"Bless the Lord, **you His angels, that excel in strength**, *that do His commandments, hearkening to the voice of His word."*
—Psalm 103:20

Before you begin this lesson, read chapter 7, " Divine Mystery #6," of 7 *Divine Mysteries.*

1. Everyone has personal thoughts and beliefs about angels. How did reading Divine Mystery #6 in the book affect your thinking and believing?

    _____

    _____

    _____

2. There is an entire class of angels known as angels of abundance. What are some of their different names, which reflect their various tasks?

    _____

    _____

    _____

3. Angels of blessing are connected to Proverbs 10:22. Write out that Scripture here in the *New King James Version*:

    _____

    _____

    _____

4. As a Christian, is it permissible for us to use our believer's authority to invite these angels to show up and pour out heavenly riches in our lives? Circle one: True or False

HAVING CHILDLIKE FAITH TO BELIEVE

5. I suggest the following prayer: "God, open the eyes of my heart. Bring me Your revelation. Give me Your wisdom in mind and spirit. Let me see the things You have available for me. Thank You for it even now." Now, write a personal and specific prayer that addresses your need today.

    _____

    _____

    _____

6. *"That the God of our Lord Jesus Christ, the Father of glory, may give to you the spirit of*

_____ _____ _____ *in the knowledge of Him: the eyes of*

your _____ *being enlightened; that you may know what is the* _____ *of*

His calling, and what the _____ *of the glory of* _____ _____ *..."*

(Ephesians 1:17–18)

7. In Genesis 28, Jacob's experience was more than a dream, and he was frightened. Yet when he realized that God was in it all, Jacob committed his life to the Lord, built a place to worship God, and pledged a tenth of his wealth.

Have you experienced "more than a dream"?

_____

_____

Were you frightened?

_____

_____

Did you discern who was behind the dream?

_____

_____

If God was in it, did you commit, build, and pledge in response?

_____

_____

THE GLORY OF GOD'S PRESENCE

8. Religious spirits are angered when believers realize they have authority over the angelic realm. How convinced are you that because Jesus lives inside you, He gives you His power and authority?

Circle one: Totally convinced – Usually – Somewhat – I need to study the Scriptures further

Write your reasoning:

_____

_____

_____

9. Why are Christians afraid of angels when they know Jesus Christ, the Hope of Glory, is living inside them? Are you afraid of angels? If so, why?

_____

_____

_____

10. List some Scriptures that confirm we are not to fear angels:

_____

_____

_____

GLORY AND ANGELS

11. To have angels working in your life, make this a focus in your prayer time with the Lord of angelic hosts. Give God prominence and yield to His authority. In this way, He will dispatch the hosts of heaven to work on your behalf. Write a prayer that embodies this mandate:

_____

_____

_____

12. As we read in the section "Angels of Abundance" in chapter 7 of *7 Divine Mysteries*: "Therefore, angels are only _____—spirits sent to _____ _____ _____ who will inherit salvation" (Hebrews 1:14 NLT).

13. If you don't believe and speak the Word, your angels are frustrated, standing idle, with nothing to act on. What aspect of God's Word will you believe and speak today in order to activate your angels?

_____

_____

_____

14. In times when you feel all alone, remember the truth that you are surrounded by a heavenly host that hovers over and around you. God's faithful servants are protecting, guarding, and watching over your life continually. Even if you can't see them working in your daily life, know that they are nevertheless present. In what ways does this assurance comfort you?

_____

_____

_____

ANGELS CLEAR THE WAY

15. What Scripture from Genesis confirms that there are angels of prosperity?

_____

16. Specific angels have been assigned to faithfully accompany you everywhere you go to give you strength and safety, and to prosper your way. Do you pay attention to the reality of angels of prosperity being assigned you? Circle one: Yes or No
If so, has it changed your thinking and your speech? If so, in what ways? If not, how can you pay closer attention to this reality?

_____

_____

_____

17. In Genesis 24:7, Abraham was very clear that an angel would go before the servant and prosper his way to find a suitable wife for Isaac. Finding the proper, godly spouse is a form of prosperity in your life. List other rich treasures that aren't found in the bank:

_____

_____

_____

18. God has angels that work in _____ _____—and we must _____ _____ _____ in our lives. When we do, we will _____ _____ new realms of _____ _____.

19. No matter what you face in life or what happens in the natural, do you believe that angels are watching over you, working with you so that you will never lack for anything?

_____

_____

_____

20. Whether you see them or not, angels of abundance are released to work in your life as you obey the voice of God's Spirit. When you move in obedience, you move with the angels and the angels move with you! In what direction are you and your angels moving today?

_____

_____

_____

ACTIVATIONS

1. Do your own research to discover how many times the word *angels* is mentioned in the Bible. In fact, you may want to search more than one Bible translation. Write down your discoveries and whether those results change your thoughts about God's messengers.

2. Pray for an angelic dream from God and then pay special attention to your dreams for the following week. Before getting out of bed, record in detail everything you remember.

3. Read my books *Seeing Angels* and *Angelic Activations* expecting new realms of abundance to open for you.

NOTES

NOTES

NOTES

NOTES

NOTES

DIVINE MYSTERY #7: GENERATIONAL INVESTING BRINGS GENERATIONAL BLESSING

"Therefore know [without any doubt] and understand that the LORD your God, He is God, the faithful God, who is keeping His covenant and His [steadfast] lovingkindness to a thousand generations with those who love Him and keep His commandments."
—Deuteronomy 7:9 (AMP)

Before you begin this lesson, read chapter 8, " Divine Mystery #7," of 7 *Divine Mysteries*.

ANSWERED PRAYERS FOR FUTURE GENERATIONS

1. After reading the story about my great-grandmother's treasures that were available for Katie's healing, did you have a new, or expanded, understanding of generational blessings?

_____

2. Jesus said, *"For where your treasure is, there your heart will be also"* (Matthew 6:21 NIV). What "treasures" do you pray for your current family and future generations to receive?

_____

_____

CHOOSE LIFE

3. *"This day I call the heavens and the earth as witnesses against you that I have set before you life and death, blessings and curses. Now _____ _____, so that you and your children may _____"* (Deuteronomy 30:19 NIV).

    You can reverse any previous generational curse by choosing life through the blood of Jesus—claiming His sacrifice for yourself and your family. (See Galatians 3:13–14.)

YOUR GENERATIONAL BLESSINGS

4. *"For we know that our _____ _____ was crucified with him* [Jesus] *so that the body ruled by sin might be done away with, that we should no longer be _____ _____ _____"* (Romans 6:6 NIV).

    Say, "The new comes now!"

NOW THE NEW COMES

5. Posturing yourself to receive generational blessings means opening your heart and hands. In what way did God bless Abraham in Genesis 24:1?

_____

    He will do the same for you and your family today and for future generations.

6. God's good work is the opposite of the enemy's evil work—and God's way prevails! Think of some opposite terms for the following:

God's Way	Satan's Way
Prosperity	_____
_____	Chaos
Health	_____
_____	Lack
Love	_____
_____	Stress

SUNSHINE IN HER SHOES

7. I mention two "golden glory" experiences. Have you had such an experience where the glory of the Lord is manifested in tangible ways? If so, write about it:

_____

_____

_____

If not yet, write what you think it will be like:

_____

_____

_____

8. God has a plan to get you through life that includes miracles, signs and wonders, and power demonstrations right when you need them. You will receive courage and boldness to act and strength to hold you up. Do you believe this? _____ Have you already received?

_____

9. Write your reaction to my story about the angel of prosperity dream and my wife's discovery on the freshly washed and dried clothes in the laundry room.

   _____

   _____

   _____

10. In faith, write out a personal decree about God's angels of prosperity filling your life:

    _____

    _____

FOUR KEYS TO OVERFLOWING ABUNDANCE

KEY #1: DECLARE THE ABUNDANCE YOU SEE IN THE SPIRIT

11. Why decree God's abundance when you see it? Job 22:28 tells us, *"You will also _____ and _____ a thing, and it will be _____ for you; and _____ _____ [_____ _____ _____] will shine upon your ways"* (AMP). Light represents God's favor, His abundance, and it will shine on you.

12. God's _____ is for your body, soul, and spirit, but you must _____ it to make it a _____ in every area of your daily life.

13. Do you believe that an angel of prosperity has been assigned to your life? _____

    If so, what have you done to declare and establish that reality?

    _____

    _____

    _____

KEY #2: ACT ON WHAT YOU SEE IN THE SPIRIT

14. When manifesting abundance, you have to first establish what you see by declaring it, and then activate it. What action did my wife and I take with the golden glory we were given, and what was the result?

_____

_____

15. James 1:21–22 says: "With a humble spirit _____ _____ _____ [_____ _____] which is implanted [actually rooted in your heart], which is able to save your souls. But prove yourselves _____ _____ _____ _____ [actively and continually obeying God's precepts], and not merely listeners [who hear the word but fail to internalize its meaning], deluding yourselves [by unsound reasoning contrary to the truth]" (AMP).

KEY #3: RECEIVE WITH THANKSGIVING WHAT YOU HAVE SEEN IN THE SPIRIT

16. Declare it, activate it, and then _____ it.

17. "For this reason I am telling you, _____ _____ _____ _____ _____ in prayer [in accordance with God's will], _____ [with confident trust] that you have received them, and they _____ _____ _____ _____ _____" (Mark 11:24 AMP).

KEY #4: SPREAD THE REVELATION

18. Why does the Bible say we should scatter our seed abroad?

_____

_____

_____

SO MUCH MORE THAN WE COULD ASK OR IMAGINE

19. When you feel something in the Spirit, _____ _____ and _____ _____.... When you receive a _____ of God's holy angels working on your behalf and you take steps to _____ the _____ they bring, that's all you need. Get hooked up to _____; you don't need any other connection.

BELIEVE GOD FOR A GENERATIONAL HARVEST

20. *"Trouble chases sinners, while **blessings reward the** _____"* (Proverbs 13:21 NLT). If *"the righteous"* describes you, take hold of the blessings! After all, Jesus says, *"Seek the Kingdom of God above all else, and live righteously, and **he will give you** _____ _____ _____"* (Matthew 6:33 NLT)!

ACTIVATIONS

1. Acknowledging that God's realm of abundance is for you and for your family, write a prayer that touches on the overflowing abundance you desire from Him. Add to the prayer every day for a week until you have a prayer that reflects your deepest, most intimate love for and worship of your heavenly Father, your Provider.
2. Buy a journal and record when you sow seeds (financial or otherwise) into an anointed ministry or reputable organization. Also record when God gives back to you multiplied abundance.
3. As the Spirit leads, take time to visit or to call members of your family and have discussions about the good things God has done in your life and what He can do for them. Keep a record of these conversations; with God's help and the Holy Spirit's guidance, begin making new decrees over your family members and expect a new wave of generational blessings.

NOTES

NOTES

NOTES

NOTES

ANSWER KEY

1: YOU CAN MANIFEST ABUNDANCE

1. What is the **environment** of divine **provision**? What are the foundational **truths** that apply to all **supernatural** mysteries of **abundance**? What clues will **unlock** their **secrets**?

2. Answers will vary. Examples of Bible passages may include these passages and/or others: Matthew 14:18–21; Exodus 16:29–32; 1 Kings 17:2–5.

3. Answers will vary.

4. Jesus was *"**looking up to heaven**, [when] He blessed and broke and gave the loaves to the disciples..."* (Matthew 14:19 NKJV).

5. Answers will vary.

6. Answers will vary. Example: True abundance is having supernatural provision to meet my spiritual, emotional, and physical needs, with enough left over to meet the needs of my family and friends. This will only happen as a result of focusing on God and worshipping Him wholeheartedly.

7. Genesis 1:28

8. *"And you shall **remember** the Lord your God, for it is He who gives you **power** to get wealth, that He may establish His covenant..."* (**Deuteronomy 8:18** NKJV).

9. Answers will vary.

10. Answers will vary.

11. Answers will vary.

12. Answers will vary. Examples: Psalm 63:5; 141:2; Lamentations 3:41

13. Answers will vary.

14. *"Who shall **ascend** into the hill of the LORD? or who shall **stand** in His holy place? He that has **clean hands**, and a **pure heart**; who has not lifted up his soul to vanity, nor sworn deceitfully"* (Psalm 24:3–4).

15. Answers will vary. Examples: cooked a meal for a friend; fixed a loose porch step; called my parent; etc.

16. Answers will vary. Examples: bitterness; unforgiveness; envy; etc.

17. When true faith is established in your heart, you can do the positive, fruitful, uplifting things that your faith dictates, which will bring abundant living.

18. The proper order that will honor God and steward His financial blessings best is: (1) Tithe/give/sow; (2) Tax; (3) Debt; (4) Save; (5) Bills; (6) Necessities; (7) Luxuries

19. This happens because when you honor the Lord and move yourself into alignment with Him through worship, the angels are there to worship with you.

20. *"Honor the LORD with your **wealth** and with the **best part** of everything you produce. Then **he will fill** your barns with grain, and your vats will **overflow** with good wine"* (Proverbs 3:9–10 NLT).

2: DIVINE MYSTERY #1

1. In this day, we must receive **heavenly vision**; when we do, instead of **perishing,** we will begin **prospering.**
2. Psalm 91:9–10 says, *"Because you have made* **the Lord,** *[who is]* **my refuge,** *even the Most High, your* **dwelling place,** *no evil will befall you, nor will any plague come near your tent"* (AMP).
3. Answers will vary. Example: "I am afraid of being alone." "I declare that I am never alone because my God is with me always. He will never leave me or forsake me!"
4. You can **break the curses** of the enemy by **standing with God** and His Word.
5. Answers will vary. Examples: shelter; house; sanctuary; retreat; home; safe haven; abode; lodging; castle; quarters; residence; hideout; port; harbor; fortress. Safety; security; protection; guarded; defended; cared for; preserved; shelter. Answers will vary.
6. Answers will vary.
7. The beautiful thing about having a **vision** is that it keeps you moving forward…. When God gives you a vision of His **abundance,** it moves us away from **lack** and toward His **overflow.** "Have you unraveled… ?": Answers will vary.
8. Angels attend to our every need. They come to **guard, protect,** and **defend** us, and they will do much more as we learn to **interact with** them and **put them to work** on our behalf.
9. Answers will vary. Examples: salvation; healing; prosperity; angels; peace; financial resources; good health; safety; hope; faith; mercy; love; grace; wisdom; riches; wealth; blessings; food; work; spiritual gifts
10. Answers will vary.
11. Answers will vary.
12. Psalm 35:27 says, *"Let them shout for* **joy** *and be* **glad,** *who favor my* **righteous cause;** *and let them say continually, 'Let* **the Lord** *be magnified, who has* **pleasure in the prosperity** *of His servant.'"*
13. Answers will vary.
14. Answers will vary. Spiritual, physical, mental, relational, financial…life abundant, with wealth of every kind.
15. Answers will vary.
16. Answers will vary.
17. *"And you shall* **remember** *the Lord your God, for it is He who gives you* **power** *to get* **wealth,** *that He may establish His covenant which He swore to your fathers, as it is this day"* (Deuteronomy 8:18 NKJV).
18. Answers will vary.
19. Answers will vary.
20. Answers will vary.

3: DIVINE MYSTERY #2

1. Answers will vary.
2. Jesus is telling us that we can have whatever we speak in faith.
3. Answers will vary.
4. *"And God* **is able** *to bless you abundantly, so that in all things at all times, having all that you need,* **you will abound** *in every good work"* (2 Corinthians 9:8 NIV).
5. Regardless of what life looks like in the natural, God has promised **victory** and **breakthroughs,** and they are available to you **right now.** "List what you are prepared for…": Answers will vary.
6. What we say **creates** a way, but what we **speak** starts in our minds and emotions.
7. Answers will vary.
8. First heaven is the atmosphere on earth; second heaven is where spiritual warfare takes place; third heaven is where God abides.
9. The third heaven, or *"heavenly places"*
10. Answers will vary.
11. Answers will vary.
12. Answers will vary. Remember, **strife** leads to lack, but **divine unity** leads to abundance. Answers to the Matthew 5:9 question will vary.
13. Answers will vary.
14. Answers will vary.
15. Answers will vary. Do you firmly believe that choosing God's truth is "the greatest spiritual warfare **weapon** you have at your disposal" and that it brings "you **victory** in **every battle**"? Answers will vary.
16. *"Then* **the Lord said** *to Joshua, 'See,* **I have delivered** *Jericho into your hands…'"* (Joshua 6:2 NIV).
17. Answers will vary.
18. Answers will vary.
19. Answers will vary.
20. Answers will vary.

4: DIVINE MYSTERY #3

1. Answers will vary.

2. Answers will vary.

3. Answers will vary. Examples of life-giving verses include (but are not limited to): Deuteronomy 30:19; Jeremiah 17:13; John 4:10; 6:63; 7:38; 10:10.

4. God's Word overcomes **stress, anxieties, worries, depression,** and **self-loathing.** His Word floods **sickness** and **disease** with **healing waters.** His Word overcomes **poverty** with the flow of **heavenly abundance.**

5. Revelation always demands **activation** to produce a manifestation.

6. God is looking for those who will *believe* His Word, *accept* the **revelation** of it, and *respond* to it…. We are to be *doers* of the Word, and in *doing the Word*—participating, working, and fully engaging with it—we will produce the *fruit* of the Word.

7. Answers will vary.

8. If you circled the word *motivate*, bravo! If you circled *intimidate*, reread Matthew 25:14–30 prayerfully.

9. Answers will vary.

10. Answers will vary.

11. Answers will vary.

12. Answers will vary.

13. Answers will vary.

14. Answers will vary.

15. Answers will vary.

16. The Holy Spirit is God, and He is infinitely higher than angels. When God created angels, He had something very special in mind for them. The truth that the Holy Spirit came into the world and endued men and women with heavenly power does not mean that angels suddenly became meaningless or obsolete.

17. We must not worship angels, pray to them, or become obsessed with them.

18. God desires to bring manifestations to your life—manifestations of **healing,** manifestations of **blessing,** manifestations of **goodness,** manifestations of **favor.** He wants to release many kinds of manifestations, but they will only come as you allow the Spirit to bring you **revelation.** There are downloads of **ideas, inventions,** and **creative abilities** waiting for you in heaven. "Will you receive these revelations…?": Answers will vary.

19. Answers will vary. Examples: Matthew 7:8; 21:22; Mark 11:24; Luke 17:6; John 16:24; James 4:3; 1 John 3:22

20. A thousand years before Jesus went to the cross, David already knew that God's Son would pay the price for our **sins to be forgiven,** that He would **heal all our diseases,** that He would **redeem our lives** from destruction, that He would **crown us** with lovingkindness and tender mercies, that He would **satisfy** our mouths with good things so that our **youth is renewed** like the eagle's.

5: DIVINE MYSTERY #4

1. Answers will vary.

2. Honor. Communication. Kindness. Peace. Gratitude. Forgiveness. Financial sacrifice.

3. Answers will vary.

4. Answers will vary. It is important to sow into good soil so the seeds can take root, mature, and produce fruit.

5. *"Good ground"* is freshly tilled and free of rocks and weeds. Another name for good ground is "God soil."

6. God **soil** with a God **seed** produces a God **harvest.** God soil is **miracle** ground that produces **miracle** results—wonderful fruitfulness and multiplication.

7. Answers will vary.

8. You can plant the Word of God as a **miracle seed** in your **heart** and then watch it grow. Over the days and weeks and months of the year in which we read the **Bible,** miracle seeds are being deposited into our **spirits,** and they are not placed there to die. They have not been planted there to get choked out by the cares of the world. God planted them with the anticipation of watching each one grow and flourish, providing a **harvest** in your life.

9. Answers will vary.

10. Answers will vary.

11. Answers will vary. Example: Good stewards allow God to use their talents, finances, and blessings any way He wants to benefit others. "When it comes to being a good "steward"…?": Answers will vary.

12. Answers will vary. Example: My gift is teaching, and I will volunteer to teach a Sunday school class to help Mary and Charles.

13. Answers will vary. Examples: I have seeds of biblical wisdom, and I will sow them by leading a Bible study. I have seeds of kindness, and I will sow them by baking cookies to share with a neighbor.

14. Answers will vary.

15. Answers will vary.

16. **Money** is an important **resource** that God wants us to have so that **His blessings** can flow to us and through us.

17. **Money** identifies the true **location** of your **heart.** *"For where your **treasure** is, there will your **heart** be also"* (Matthew 6:21).

18. **Money** should always be used to **serve God,** who is the Source of overflowing abundance.

19. **Money** is a tool for **global harvest.**

20. **Money** always **exposes** a **poverty spirit**. *"…remember the* LORD *your God, for it is He who* **gives you** *the power to get* **wealth***…"* (Deuteronomy 8:18 NKJV).

6: DIVINE MYSTERY #5

1. **Giving** and then **generously receiving** from God's abundance go hand in hand.
2. Answers will vary.
3. Answers will vary. Examples: Psalm 23:1; 68:35; Nehemiah 9:21; Ecclesiastes 2:26; John 6:33; James 1:5
4. Answers will vary.
5. Answers will vary.
6. Out of the overflow of God's **love** for you, He wants to **shower you** with abundance. I urge you to accept **His gifts** with **joy**, praise, and **thanksgiving**.
7. Answers will vary.
8. Answers will vary.
9. Answers will vary.
10. Our God is the Spirit of **Generosity**, and He wants the realm of **His abundance** to flow in and **through your life** every day.
11. The Hebrew word *kabod* literally means "weight."
12. Answers will vary.
13. Answers will vary. Example: Children don't overanalyze and dissect God's blessings; in contrast to adults, they willingly accept them and release them.
14. God wants you to be a **generous receiver** so you can then be an extraordinary, extravagant, and **generous giver** too.
15. Answers will vary.
16. Answers will vary.
17. Level 6 speaks of **spiritual** and **financial** prosperity, as well as of divine **favor**, **appointments**, and **connections**.
18. Answers will vary.
19. *"So let's not get tired of* **doing** *what is* **good***. At just the right time we will* **reap** *a harvest of* **blessing** *if we* **don't give up"** (Galatians 6:9 NLT).
20. I can keep moving forward in the Spirit by giving, receiving, releasing, receiving, and giving again.

7: DIVINE MYSTERY #6

1. Answers will vary.
2. Some different names for angels of abundance are: angels of blessing, angels of provision, angels of finance and favor, and angels of prosperity.
3. Proverbs 10:22: *"The blessing of the* LORD *makes one rich, and He adds no sorrow with it"* (NKJV).
4. True
5. Answers will vary.
6. *"That the God of our Lord Jesus Christ, the Father of glory, may give to you the spirit of* **wisdom and revelation** *in the knowledge of Him: the eyes of your* **understanding** *being enlightened; that you may know what is the* **hope** *of His calling, and what the* **riches** *of the glory of* **His inheritance***…"* (Ephesians 1:17–18).
7. Answers will vary.
8. Answers will vary.
9. Answers will vary.
10. Answers will vary. Examples: Genesis 21:17; Psalm 91:11; Matthew 1:20; 28:5; Mark 16:17; Luke 1:13, 30; 2:10
11. Answers will vary.
12. *"Therefore, angels are only* **servants***—spirits sent to* **care for people** *who will inherit salvation"* (Hebrews 1:14 NLT).
13. Answers will vary.
14. Answers will vary. Example: It brings me peace of mind and calms my spirit.
15. Genesis 24:40: *"He said to me, 'The* LORD*, before whom I walk, will send His angel with you and prosper your way'"* (NKJV).
16. Answers will vary.
17. Answers will vary.
18. God has angels that work in **mysterious ways**—and we must **welcome their ministry** in our lives. When we do, we will **walk in** new realms of **divine abundance**.
19. Answers will vary.
20. Answers will vary.

8: DIVINE MYSTERY #7

1. Answers will vary.
2. Answers will vary.

3. *"This day I call the heavens and the earth as witnesses against you that I have set before you life and death, blessings and curses. Now **choose life**, so that you and your children may **live"** (Deuteronomy 30:19 NIV).

4. *"For we know that our **old self** was crucified with him [Jesus] so that the body ruled by sin might be done away with, that we should no longer be **slaves to sin"*** (Romans 6:6 NIV).

5. *"In all things"*

6. Answers will vary. Examples: opposite of prosperity: poverty; opposite of chaos: order, function; opposite of health: sickness; opposite of lack: abundance; opposite of stress: peace.

7. Answers will vary.

8. Answers will vary.

9. Answers will vary.

10. Answers will vary.

11. *"You will also **decide** and **decree** a thing, and it will be **established** for you; and **the light [of God's favor]** will shine upon your ways"* (AMP).

12. God's **abundance** is for your body, soul, and spirit, but you must **access** it to make it a **reality** in every area of your daily life.

13. Answers will vary.

14. They placed it in multiple envelopes with little pieces of cloth, prayed over them, and then sent them out to people around the world who had written for prayer—as modeled in Acts 19:11–12. God did many miracles.

15. James 1:21–22 says: *"With a humble spirit **receive the word [of God]** which is implanted [actually rooted in your heart], which is able to save your souls. But prove yourselves **doers of the word** [actively and continually obeying God's precepts], and not merely listeners [who hear the word but fail to internalize its meaning], deluding yourselves [by unsound reasoning contrary to the truth]"* (AMP).

16. Declare it, activate it, and then **embrace** it.

17. *"For this reason I am telling you, **whatever things you ask for** in prayer [in accordance with God's will], **believe** [with confident trust] that you have received them, and they **will be given to you"*** (Mark 11:24 AMP).

18. We should scatter our seed abroad because we have no way of knowing which field will produce the most.

19. When you feel something in the Spirit, **say it** and **pray it**.... When you receive a **revelation** of God's holy angels working on your behalf and you take steps to **receive** the **blessings** they bring, that's all you need. Get hooked up to **heaven**; you don't need any other connection.

20. *"Trouble chases sinners, while **blessings reward the righteous"*** (Proverbs 13:21 NLT). If *"the righteous"* describes you, take hold of the blessings! After all, Jesus says, *"Seek the Kingdom of God above all else, and live righteously, and **he will give you everything you need"*** (Matthew 6:33 NLT)!

RECOMMENDED RESOURCES

Other Books by Joshua Mills

31 Days of Health, Wealth & Happiness

31 Days to a Breakthrough Prayer Life

31 Days to a Miracle Mindset

Angelic Activations: A Scriptural Look at the Modern-Day Ministry of Angels

Atmosphere: Creating a Realm for Miracles & Success

*Creative Glory: Embracing the Realm of Divine Expression**

The Glory: Scriptures & Prayers to Manifest God's Presence in Your Life

*Moving in Glory Realms: Exploring Dimensions of Divine Presence**

Positioned for Prosperity: Unlocking the Realms of Blessing, Favor & Increase

The Power of His Names (77 devotional cards and guidebook)

*Power Portals: Awaken Your Connection to the Spirit Realm**

*Seeing Angels: How to Recognize and Interact with Your Heavenly Messengers**

Simple Supernatural: Keys to Living in the Glory Realm

Third Day Prayers

Time & Eternity: Taking Authority Over Your Day!

Albums by Joshua Mills (CD or Digital Download)

Activating Angels in Your Life (2-disc CD)

Experience His Glory

Opening the Portals (2-disc CD)

Power Prayers

Reversing the Clock

SpiritSpa (instrumental piano)

SpiritSpa 2

*Also available: audiobook and study guide

Joshua Mills's resources are available online at:
www.JoshuaMills.com

ABOUT THE AUTHOR

Joshua Mills is an internationally recognized, ordained minister of the gospel, as well as a recording artist and keynote conference speaker. He has also authored more than twenty books and training manuals. His books with Whitaker House include *7 Divine Mysteries*, *Power Portals*, *Moving in Glory Realms*, and *Seeing Angels*, all with corresponding study guides and audiobooks, and *Angelic Activations*.

Joshua is well known for the supernatural atmosphere that he carries and for his unique insights into the glory realm and prophetic sound. Wherever Joshua ministers, the Word of God is confirmed by miraculous signs and wonders that testify of Jesus Christ. He is regarded as a spiritual forerunner in the body of Christ. For many years, he has helped people discover the life-shifting truths of salvation, healing, and deliverance for spirit, soul, and body.

Joshua and his wife, Janet, cofounded International Glory Ministries and have ministered in over seventy-five nations on six continents. Featured together in several film documentaries and print articles, they have ministered to millions around the world through radio, television, and their weekly webcast, *Glory Bible Study*. They live with their three children, Lincoln, Liberty, and Legacy, and their puppy, Buttercup.

www.JoshuaMills.com

Welcome to Our House!

We Have a Special Gift for You

It is our privilege and pleasure to share in your love of Christian books. We are committed to bringing you authors and books that feed, challenge, and enrich your faith.

To show our appreciation, we invite you to sign up to receive a specially selected **Reader Appreciation Gift**, with our compliments. Just go to the Web address at the bottom of this page.

God bless you as you seek a deeper walk with Him!

[WE HAVE A GIFT FOR YOU. VISIT:]

whpub.me/nonfictionthx

WHITAKER
HOUSE